ADVENTIST PIONEER SERIES

WILLIAM MILLER
tells the world

Written by
MONIK FOLKMAN

Illustrated by
LOLA USUPOVA

Copyright © 2025 Butter n' Honey
ISBN 978-1-967145-03-4

Illustrated by Lola Usupova
Edited by Rebecca McKinney

Scriptures quoted are from King James Version.
Direct quotes are from *Memoirs of William Miller* by Sylvester Bliss.
Image used is in public domain, author unknown.

More books are coming soon! Go to www.adventistpioneerseries.com.

"I have fixed my mind on another time, and here I mean to stand until God gives me more light, and that is, today, today, and today, until He comes...."

— William Miller

William Miller was an American farmer known for saying that Jesus was coming very soon. His message caused a great spiritual revival in America in the mid-1800s, and many people surrendered their hearts to Jesus.

However, preaching to the world was not always easy for William.

As a young boy, William was eager to learn and loved to read. There were only three books in his house—a Bible, a Psalter, and a book of prayers.

After reading them over and over,
he borrowed more books from his neighbors.

His love of reading made William creative—and unfortunately, disobedient. Working all day on the farm, William wanted to use his free time at night to read. But his parents needed to save money, so they refused to buy him candles and forbade him from staying up late for fear he would be too tired to work the next day.

William came up with an idea to use pine knots as a way to rekindle the fire downstairs after everyone had gone to sleep. He collected the pine knots during the day, cut them to the right size, and hid them. This way, William secretly enjoyed many books for hours into the night.

One night, he got caught! His father woke up thinking the house was on fire—only to find William reading a book. His father warned him that if he didn't go to bed right away, there would be consequences!

After he was married, William no longer had to sneak around at night to read. His wife, Lucy, encouraged his love of reading by doing more work around the farm so he could go to the library.

William made friends and read many books. However, some of the books and friends he encountered were not good influences, as they pointed out what seemed like contradictions in the Bible.

But through different circumstances in his life, God still reached out to William's doubtful heart. Once he found the Savior and became a Christian, William's love of reading helped him grow quickly in his faith.

He decided to study the Bible for himself until he could make sense of his friends' contradictions. This is how he studied the Bible: he started with the book of Genesis and read verse by verse. He did not move on until he understood each verse. He compared scripture with scripture using only the marginal references and the concordance.

In 1818, two years after he began studying his Bible—specifically the longest-time prophecy in the book of Daniel, known as the 2300-day prophecy—William concluded that Jesus would return in 1843. However, he hesitated to share his solemn conclusion, fearing that other Christians might become too excited about his findings without studying for themselves. Instead, he studied for five more years to ensure he had the right interpretation.

But once he was fully convinced his interpretation was correct, William became heavily burdened to share it with others.

"Go and tell the world of their danger"

rang daily in his heart as he worked on the farm. And the words of the prophet Ezekiel kept coming back to him, saying, "If though dost not speak to warn the wicked from his way, that wicked man shall die in his iniquity; but his blood will I require at thine hand."

William tried sharing his interpretation with a few friends and family, but that did not make the burdening voice go away.

One August morning in 1833, the voice bid him stronger than ever:
"Go and tell it to the world."

"I can't go, Lord," was William's answer.

When the Lord asked him why not, William replied, "I am not used to speaking to a lot of people. I am not fit for this work!" Though William's excuses made sense, the burden did not go away. So, finally, he made a promise.

He promised that if he received an invitation to speak publicly, he would accept the Lord's request to share his message with others. This promise relieved William because he thought it was unlikely to happen.

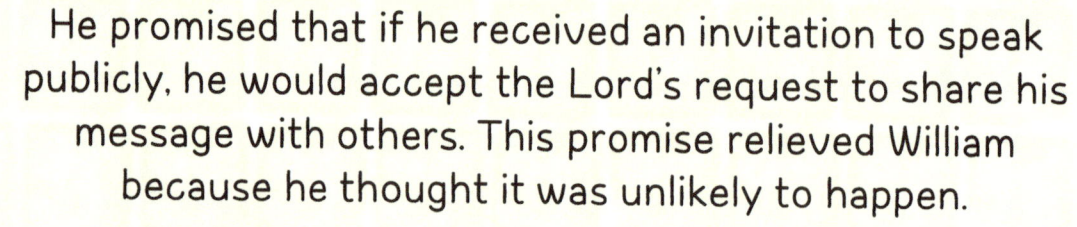

However, half an hour later, to William's great surprise, his nephew came knocking on the door with a message. The church was without a preacher for the next day, and the nephew's father requested that William come and preach about the Lord's coming!

Stunned by the invitation, William felt angry with himself for making such a promise and hurried to a grove of maple trees nearby to wrestle with God about it. An hour later, the thought, "Will you make a covenant with God, and break it so soon?" was impressed upon his mind. So William finally submitted, willing to go.

The next day, William preached his first sermon on the Lord's soon coming. His fear melted away, and he was able to speak well. The message captivated the people so much that they asked William to stay and preach for another week.

People from nearby towns came, and a revival sprung up. Thirteen families, all except two people, were converted!

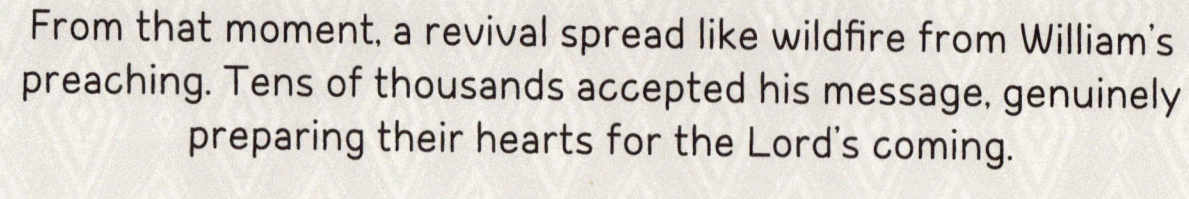

From that moment, a revival spread like wildfire from William's preaching. Tens of thousands accepted his message, genuinely preparing their hearts for the Lord's coming.

As people came together to pray almost every hour, places that once sold alcohol or hosted gambling shut down and turned into meeting rooms.

Unfortunately, those who did not accept William's message mocked those who did.

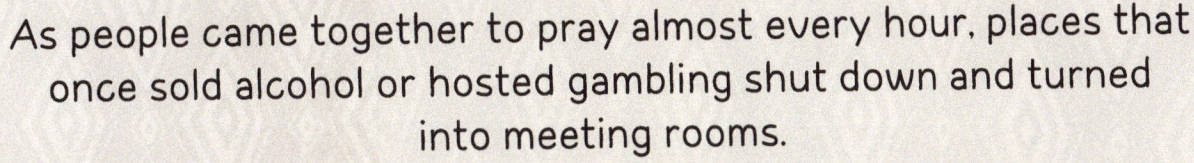

From his study, William determined that the Lord would return sometime between 1843 and 1844. A man named Samuel Snow discovered the exact date, October 22, 1844, during his personal study.

That day came, but the Lord did not come. Many were greatly disappointed. Only a few stayed and continued to study the 2300-day prophecy.

Though it may have looked like a defeat, William's work was not in vain. Unknown to him, his interpretation was right on the date but not on the event, as it was not about Jesus' second coming, and his message would result in another great movement.

No doubt, it was a discouraging experience for William. However, his faith never wavered. Later, he wrote,

"I have fixed my mind on another time, and here I mean to stand until God gives me more light, and that is, today, today, today until He comes."

Like William, you may find God's calling hard to follow. But if you surrender, you will find the task light. As William discovered, whenever He calls you to do something, He also gives you the strength to do it—all you have to do is just believe His word.

"Faithful is he that calleth you, who also will do it."
1 Thessalonians 5:24

WILLIAM MILLER

February 15, 1782
William Miller was born in Pittsfield, Massachusetts.

1786
William and his family moved to Low Hampton, New York. This was the place where William grew up. He was homeschooled by his mother until the age of nine and then attended East Poultney School District.

He did not receive formal schooling after the age of 18.

June 29, 1803
William married Lucy Smith. Afterwards, the newlyweds moved to Poultney, Vermont. They had ten children, eight of whom lived to adulthood.

July 21, 1810
William was commissioned as a lieutenant in the army.

February 1, 1814
William was promoted to captain by the President of the United States.

September 11, 1814
The Battle of Plattsburgh commenced. This battle was part of the War of 1812, and it was the battle that ended the British invasion of the northern states of the United States. This battle was one of the turning points in William Miller's conversion.

June 18, 1815
William was discharged from the army and returned to Poultney.

September 1816
William was converted after listening to a sermon by a doctor who preached before the celebration of the anniversary of the Battle of Plattsburgh, and on the next day, while reading a sermon at church, he received a vivid impression of the Savior. He soon started studying the Bible.

1818
William made a solemn conclusion that Jesus was to come again sometime between March 21st, 1843, and March 21st, 1844, according to the Jewish calendar from his study of the 2300-day prophecy. He was reluctant to share his study and kept studying to make sure he had the right interpretation.

1823
William started to feel the burden to share with others, but still feeling hesitant, he only shared with friends and acquaintances.

August 1833
William made a promise to God that he would preach on Jesus's coming upon invitation only. To his surprise, he received an invitation half an hour later. The next day, he preached his first sermon on the topic in a town called Dresden.

Spring 1843
Jesus did not come as William predicted. William and others who followed his message, called the Millerites, were disappointed.

August 1844
Samuel Snow presented a corrected date of Jesus's coming which would be on October 22, 1844.

October 22, 1844
Jesus did not come, and there was a great disappointment among the Millerites.

December 20, 1849
William Miller died in full faith that Jesus would return soon.

February 15, 1782 - December 20, 1849

Have you read this one?

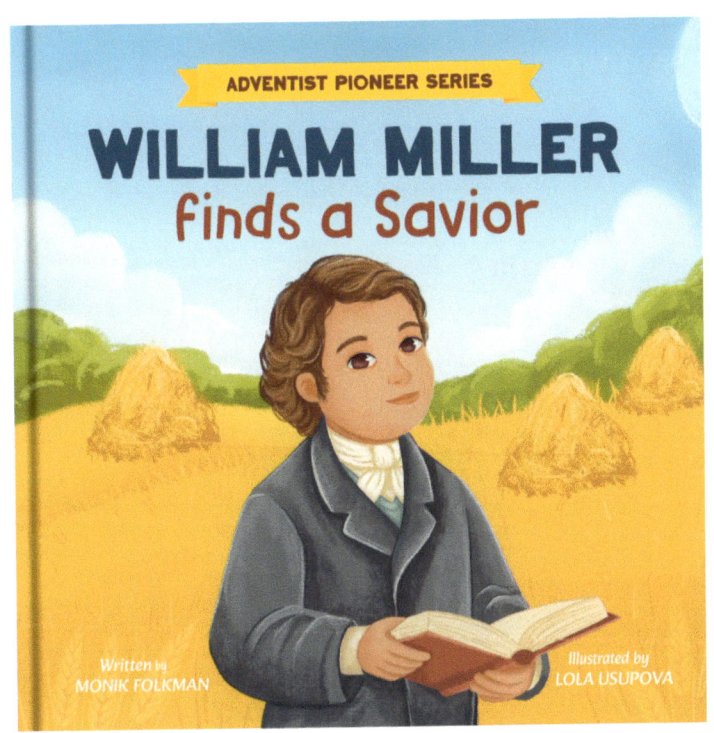

www.adventistpioneerseries.com

www.ingramcontent.com/pod-product-compliance
Lightning Source LLC
Chambersburg PA
CBHW041436120626
46547CB00002B/239